On Holy Ground
A Guide to the Ecclesiastical Sites of
Westray and ▲ Papa Westray

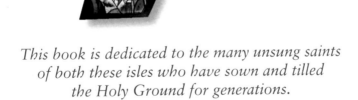

*This book is dedicated to the many unsung saints
of both these isles who have sown and tilled
the Holy Ground for generations.*

CREDITS

Project Management
and advertising: Myra Kent
Research: Sam Harcus, Iain MacDonald
Additional research (Papay)   Jocelyn Rendall
Text: Iain MacDonald
Photos: Peter Needham, Jocelyn Rendall,
Iain MacDonald
Westray Heritage Centre p19
George Burgher p25
Graham Maben p62

Funders: Westray Community Council
Papay Community Council
 Orkney Islands Council
The Kirk Session of Westray Parish Kirk
for providing the loan which made this
publication possible

Designed by Peter Needham
Typeset in Sabon Light, Sabon Light Italic and Helvetica Neue

Published by Seabridge, Furrigarth House, Westray, Orkney, KW17 2DW
on behalf of MS Research, Westray, Orkney
Printed by Ambassador Litho Ltd, Bristol
August 2006
ISBN10 0-9553667-0-4
ISBN13 978-0-9553667-0-3

CONTENTS

*Thanks to the many who read over the text, assisted with research,
dug deep into memory, and offered valuable guidance.*

With special thanks to:

George Burgher
Kathleen Drever
Marjorie Drever
Denis Fergus
Sarah Jane Gibbon
Stuart Gray
Helen Lumsden
Graham Maben
Jo MacDonald
Jocelyn Rendall
Billy Seatter
Tammo Seatter
Nancy Scott
Catherine Stevenson
Wilma Stout

Westray Heritage Centre.

Visit the Tourist Association web site for information about our arts and crafts, heritage, wildlife and where to stay, eat, drink, shop and worship.

Enquiry line: 01857 677777

www.westrayandpapawestray.com

INTRODUCTION

Be still,
For the presence of the Lord,
The Holy One is here;
Come bow before him now
With reverence and fear:
In him no sin is found –
we stand on Holy ground.
Be still,
for the presence of the Lord,
the Holy one, is here".
(David J. Evans)

This modest book has two purposes. The obvious one is to bring together the story of the Christian heritage of both Westray and Papay. In doing so we've relied upon a number of sources (listed in bibliography) and are hugely indebted to many of these sources and their authors. Indeed, you're unlikely to find any startlingly new revelations here. But it's the first time that all this information has been compiled into one volume.

We hope it will be of interest to locals and visitors alike. It has been designed as a guidebook for those who want to visit the places listed and to learn more about them. But it's also intended as an aid to contemplation and challenge for those who wish to think on the significance of this rich heritage. As such, a short reflective thought and prayer forms part of each main account.

In dealing with ancient sites it's inevitable that some issues are speculative but we've endeavoured throughout to differentiate between the possible (or even probable) and the verifiably factual.

The other main purpose of the book is quite simply to raise funds. Multiple Sclerosis (MS) is a disabling condition which affects these isles disproportionately. Many thousands of pounds have already been raised here to help in the efforts to find a cure for an illness that could and should be a thing of the past. Every penny raised will go towards that vital goal.

If you wish to make a further contribution towards MS Research there are details on the back cover of how you can do so.

We realise that most of our advertisers will see this as a way to support the cause rather than some unmissable commercial opportunity! We're very grateful for their support and for yours in buying the book.

WESTRAY & PAPAY

WESTRAY AND PAPA WESTRAY *(or Papay) are two of Orkney's northernmost isles and, like all of Orkney, are mind-blowingly rich in ancient sites. Despite their comparatively modest size (Westray is about 13 miles N to S and 5 miles at its widest, Papay a mere 3½ miles long by 1 mile across) there is a staggering number of antiquarian sites of national and international significance.*

With unbroken habitation spanning at least 6,000 years we can safely assume that the basic human need for worship has been met throughout

that time. But ancient history, though giving many tentative clues, is unable to reveal much of substance about the pagan faith of our ancestors. What is evident, particularly from the monuments they left, is that ritual played a major role in their lives and that an understanding of the cycles of life was of huge significance to them. New archaeological finds regularly provide further clues but these remain tiny fragments of the wider picture and the reality is that any theological understanding of their religious practices remains firmly in the field of assumption and imagination.

This book therefore deals exclusively with our Christian heritage, and in particular with the places of worship in which people have found spiritual sustenance, challenge, and meaning over the past one and a half millenia.

Today both isles are served by several congregations whose current places of worship are all covered here.

For further information on all that Westray and Papay have to offer visit Westray & Papa Westray Tourist Association at www.westrayandpapawestray.com or Westray Development Trust at www.westray-orkney.co.uk

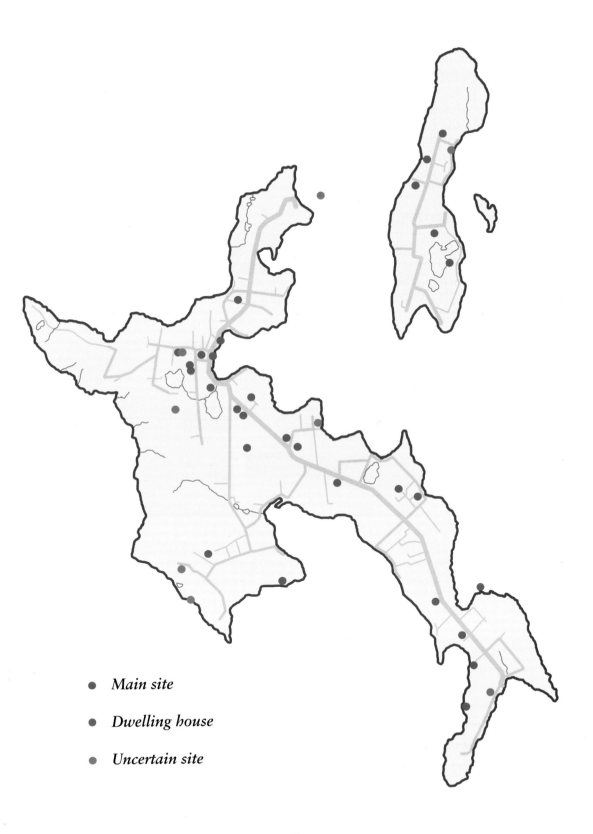

●   *Main site*

●   *Dwelling house*

●   *Uncertain site*

BAPTIST KIRK

HY 435 485

DIRECTIONS:
Heading north through Pierowall village, turn left immediately before the Gospel Hall, opposite the Royal Bank and you'll see the Kirk straight ahead at the top of a rise. There's actually a small blue sign on the main road to point the way and "Baptist Kirk" fixed in large letters above the porch, so you've no excuse for missing it! There's no hard standing but plenty room to park. Entrance is by the doors on either side of the porch.

HISTORY:
Dedicated in 1850, following the gift of land from one of the local Deacons, the new Church replaced the increasingly inadequate "tabernacle" at The Vestray (see page 33). The Manse was built around the same time at the foot of the brae. It was extended in 1985 and was in use as the Baptist Manse until sold in 2006.

Externally, the Kirk building is like a smaller version of the Church of Scotland (see page 12) with its part-piended roof and harled walls. The outside has remained relatively unchanged with the obvious exception of the little hall and vestry built on to the south end in 1906. This was further extended to the west with a kitchen and toilets in 1979. More recently, in 2005, some structural repairs and a complete re-roofing were carried out.

Inside, the layout is tight and simple with the single block of fixed pews (centrally divided) reaching up the slightly tiered floor to the rear wall. The preponderance of richly dark wood gives a warm and homely feeling. There is no grand pulpit or ornate fittings – just a modest and homely place of worship.

There's a wonderful historical record to be found on some of the old pew shelves, particularly to the rear, where generations of names and other fascinating graffiti have been carved into the surface.

COMMENT:

The building itself is modest rather than monumental but like all places of authentic worship, the Church is the people not the shell in which they gather. And this is a Church that has done much to shape not just the lives of its own members but the ecclesiastical map of Orkney. As the first Baptist Church in Orkney, the congregation "planted" several others throughout the county (of which the larger Kirkwall congregation still thrives) and through the likes of preaching, music ministries and youth outreach can be seen to have punched above their weight.

This was achieved against a historical set-back (see page 18) when two thirds of the membership left to form another denomination, an event which would have fatally demoralised many congregations. As in most such rifts; families were split apart, loyalties strained to their limits, and the sense of betrayal was strong. The trauma felt by those leaving the fold would have been equally harrowing.

There is an obvious parable of life and faith here, a message of resilience and the ability to rebuild after a seemingly hopeless situation. The parallel with bereavement and other personal tragedies needs little elaboration. Suffice to say that the light shines in the darkness and the darkness can never put it out.

REFLECTION:

The human ability to recover from despair is a constant source of amazement to me. That people can find that life is worth living again, following the most dreadful of losses is truly miraculous in every sense.

Christ who wept,
Christ who suffered,
Christ who died,
May we know you in the depth of our darkness.

Christ who rose,
Christ who lives,
Christ triumphant,
May we know you in the glory of your light.

Amen.

The Kirk is always open.

Services at 11.30am every Sunday. Evening services variable.

CASTLE O' BURRIAN

HY 503 429

CAR PARK

DIRECTIONS:

About a mile or so north of the Rapness pier you'll see a heritage (brown) sign for "Castle O' Burrian" pointing east along a side road. Take this turning and park at the area by the old mill. From here you need to follow the cliff-top path for about 300 yards until you're facing the rock stack. There's a box at the first gate for donations to help local heritage projects.

HISTORY:

Those who come searching for a fortified castle or stately home will be disappointed. Those who come with their spiritual imagination laid open will find it broadened yet further.

The "castle" is actually a sea stack. It's unadvisable to climb it without local guidance but if you do reach the top you'll find a very uneven, spongy surface, undermined by decades of puffin activity. There are remains of two small rounded structures on the west-side of the summit and a probable third to the NE of the stack where some walling and loose stones can be seen. All of these earth and stone remains are now covered in turf so even their outline is undetectable from the neighbouring slopes.

The buildings have long been assumed to be an early Christian hermitage site and have been compared to similar at the Brough of Deerness (there are other probable sites off the coasts of Hoy and Stronsay). Unless (or until) a more thorough examination is carried out this has to remain speculative but such a suggestion is quite probable and not just because it's hard to think of any other explanation.

There are many examples elsewhere of sea-faring hermits who were sent out from monastic centres (particularly Iona) to seek a life of ascetic solitude. They reached as far north as the Faroe Isles, Iceland, and quite possibly further (with some evidence of Arctic journeys to

Spitsbergen and Greenland), living in caves or building simple bowed-wall cells in almost inaccessible places.

St. Columba's biographer, Adomnán, records that an Irish monk named Cormac was in Orkney before the end of the 6th century. If this is such a location then it could easily date as far back as that, making it Westray's earliest known Christian site … probably!

COMMENT:

These were not evangelists or missionaries in the sense we use today but people who lived well apart from everyone else in a life of hermitic prayer. Asceticism is a strange concept for most of us today. Did Jesus spend so much of his time living and working with the most discarded and rejected of society in order that his followers should run away from the same desperate needs? Put like that it sounds more like selfish escapism than faithful discipleship.

But these were different times and there were new horizons to be explored as well as the work of others to be supported in prayer. It was also strongly believed that personal suffering brought believers closer into solidarity and understanding with Christ himself. It's hard to imagine just what an act of courage and faith it must have been to launch out on your own into the totally unknown and uncharted in a simple boat made from little more than wood and skins.

Their depth of faith and sense of vocation is something to truly marvel at. That we tend not to understand service in this way now, does not mean that we can't admire those who once did.

REFLECTION:

There is no Christian granted an exemption certificate. All are called into service. Even the most frail and least able have an essential ministry of prayer which they can fulfil. It is vital and should never be under-valued.

Lord,
In stillness let us hear your voice.
In solitude let us feel your presence.
In prayer let us know your will...

...and may we be stirred into service accordingly.

Amen.

CHURCH OF SCOTLAND
(Westray Parish Kirk)

HY 494 426

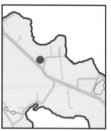

DIRECTIONS:

Known locally as the Old Kirk and sitting atop the hill at Kirkbrae, this is a landmark of some prominence. If you're heading north from Rapness on the island's main road, the B9066, you'll meet it on the right hand side at the turning for Cleaton House, about 1½ miles south of Pierowall. There is ample parking space on three sides and the building always stands open.

HISTORY:

Opened in 1846, the building has been extensively renovated and restored in recent years and was rededicated in 2002. This followed a lengthy and determined campaign by the congregation to raise a total of over £200,000 through a combination of generous giving and determined effort.

From the outside you see a tall barn-like shape with a part-piended roof in local flagstone. There is a small room (former vestry) attached to the north west and a porch (main entrance) with its little stained glass window at the south east. Thanks to the recent re-harling, the exterior appears little changed over 160 years.

Inside, however, it's a different story and is a delightful surprise for many. There are several rooms (including the large sanctuary) which offer fully flexible space and are home to many community groups and activities. The main hall / sanctuary is dominated by the original (and restored) pulpit. Everything else, including one of Orkney's few real pipe organs, is flexible and easily moveable. There is a stair lift to make the upstairs room and balcony more accessible.

Of particular pride to the congregation are the ground source heat-pump, wind turbine and bio-diesel generator, making Westray Parish Kirk the first in the country to meet all its primary heating needs from renewable sources. Along with its sister-congregation in Papay (see page 42) it was amongst the first Churches in the country to qualify for an Eco-Congregation award.

COMMENT:

This is a building which is now geared up for day-to-day multi-purpose use. The rooms are well furnished, the ancillary spaces (kitchen, toilets etc.) are more than adequate and there's a good standard of equipment throughout. In other words it's equipped for fellowship. And so it should be.

It's sometimes said that worship is central to the life of a congregation – too true. But so are things like pastoral concern, Christian education, appropriate outreach and a sense of direction. All are vital. And so is fellowship.

We read in the New Testament how members of the early Christian Church shared their time, their talents, even their possessions with one another. When they met for worship they did so around a meal – not sharing small amounts of bread and wine in a purely sacramental way – but a full meal shared together as the central focus of their praise.

We should never devalue the importance of fellowship in the life of a congregation. It strengthens our sense of togetherness and creates bonds upon which the other aspects of congregational life can be built.

Jesus said that others would gauge our level of discipleship by how much love we have for each other. That love is most clearly shown in our commitment to meaningful fellowship.

REFLECTION:
Have a look round the inside of the Kirk and enjoy the (usually!) calm atmosphere. Remember that in the centre of all the activities that take place here remains a group of people trying to be servants and followers. Give thanks for that.

Jesus,
You walked and talked with us,
You stopped and sat down with us,
You visited our house,
You joined in our party,
You cooked fish for us,
You broke bread for us,
You poured wine for us,
Thank you for the gift of sharing
And for the light of your example.
Amen.

A booklet titled *Labour of Love* explaining about the history and recent renovation is available in the Kirk.

A free leaflet gives information on the facilities and equipment.

The building is always open and visitors are welcome at any time.

Services at 11.30am every Sunday
Evening services variable.

CROSS KIRK

HY 455 431

DIRECTIONS:
Head south from Pierowall on the B9067 (Westside road). About ¼ mile past the Midbea Schoolhouse and junction (on the left) you'll reach a T junction, where the main road veres to the right (west). Turn east here past the farm of Tuquoy and follow the road south round the shore until you reach a parking area (O/S ref : HY 459 436). From hear you need to follow the coastline path round the shore for about ½ mile until you arrive at the Kirk.

HISTORY:
Haflidi Thorkelsson is credited with the building of this Kirk, which takes its name from its dedication to the Holy Cross, some time early to mid 12th century.

It was originally made up of a small nave (west) and a chancel (east). The extent of the original nave can still be clearly seen (flagstone floor). This was more than doubled to the west in a later extension (now gravel floor). Surprisingly it's the older part that is best preserved. One arched door and window remain in the south wall and part of the vaulted chancel roof is still intact. It is said that there was originally a window in the east wall of the chancel.

The whole building is enclosed by a cemetery, containing some very old graves and many of those buried here will have been residents of the sizeable and important Viking settlement, which lay just a little round the coast to the west. The heavy rate of coastal erosion suggests that the original site would have been some way back from the shore.

The Cross Kirk survived the Reformation and was used as a Parish Kirk until sometime around 1776/7. It is currently in the custodianship of Historic Scotland.

COMMENT:
To the untrained eye (such as this writer's) this is little more than an interesting and pretty ruin within an old burial ground. To those with more of an archaeological background this is one of Orkney's best preserved 12th century Kirks, dating from a period which holds many unanswered questions, and giving significant clues as to the ecclesiastical organisation and architecture of the time. As such, it is considered as a site of national (and even international) significance.

Some distance from the nearest house, it now appears to be on the very edge of community but was once right beside a high-status Viking era settlement where people lived, worked, traded and evidently, worshipped.

For over 600 years this building saw Baptisms, funerals and all stages of human experience that lie between. And in all that time this was a place where God was praised and where answers to the deepest questions of life and love were sought. As in all Church communities, tragedy and triumph, despair and delight would have been known in equal measure ... for over 600 years.

This is no small thing. Remember that even the oldest Church building in use by any of the current congregations (in either Westray or Papay) has only stood for a mere quarter of that time.

REFLECTION:
"Rock of ages, cleft for me"

Concepts of distance and time
Are merely our finite way
of trying to make sense of what's infinite.
...generations and centuries for us
...the momentary blink of a divine eye for you.

It's a breathtaking notion, Lord,
That through all these ages
Your love for your people endures,
Not abstract but personal
A rock of ages, cleft for me,
Even for me.

Amen.

EAST KIRK

HY 456 461

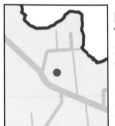

DIRECTIONS:

If travelling by car the best place to park is at the Parish Kirk (see page 12) and walk down the road towards Rapness. About 50 yards or so on the left hand side you'll come to the track that leads to the cottage of Wurrus (formerly known as the East Session House), which is currently in use as a holiday home and often has people staying. Obviously, their privacy should be respected.

HISTORY:

This was the site of a sizeable, if rather short-lived, Kirk which was built to replace the crumbling Cross Kirk (see page 14) around 1776/7. It is referred to as the East Parish Church, which is rather confusing because the Parish title was actually "West" for most of that time (see Comment). Even more confusingly, it appears that the new building, though three miles away, was also sometimes referred to as the Cross Kirk.

Old maps show that it was built right on what was then the main route down to Cleat. In 1845 the bold decision was made to build a bigger and better structure close by (the current Parish Kirk) and the East Kirk became surplus to need when the new building opened in December 1846.

It's said that the stone was used to build the dykes around Cleat's fields, which still dominate the landscape today.

Immediately in front (SE) of the cottage the walls of a large enclosure can be clearly traced. These are the likely foundation walls of the Kirk. The cottage itself was used as a meeting place for the Kirk Session and probably for other meetings such as Sunday School and Bible Study. This arrangement of a nearby or adjoining Session House was quite common in rural Churches of the era.

COMMENT:

Of all the sites featured in this booklet, this one proved the most difficult to determine. Whilst some clues emerged from various documents, there is barely a mention in most of the more weighty studies and surveys. With few visible clues and some confusion over parish names, building names, and geographical references this one taxed our very basic detective skills to their limit.

Prior to formally unifying as one administrative parish, Westray comprised two separate administrative parishes (for many years Papay was a third, which for ecclesiastical purposes also came under Westray). Although referred to as parishes they were all within the one parochial charge which was the responsibility of one minister. The two administrative parishes were North (which basically covered the districts of Aikerness, Rackwick, Dykeside and Pierowall) and West (covering Westside, Cleat, Skelwick and Rapness).

When the Cross Kirk (very much in the Westside) was deteriorating the decision was made to replace it with a larger building on the more populous (east) side of the West Parish. The name "East" appears to refer to the location within the parish rather than the actual parish title. Clear as mud?

REFLECTION:

"Whatever is hidden away will be brought out into the open, and whatever is covered up will be uncovered". (Mark 4:22, GNB).

I've frequently quoted an elderly Westray woman who commented on the death of her husband by saying, "He kens the great secret noo". These aren't fickle words. They're words of remarkable insight and faith.

So much, Lord, is unknown,
Unexplained,
Draped in the great veil.

We're drawn to the numinous
Attracted to the hidden
Anxious to unravel the mystery.

Grant us faith amidst our intellectual yearning.
Slake our inquisitiveness with trust
And teach us to hunger and thirst for righteousness
With similar zeal.

Amen.

GOSPEL HALL

HY 437 485

DIRECTIONS:
Very much in the centre of Pierowall, the hall abuts the road and stands opposite the Royal Bank at the entrance to the Baptist Kirk (see page 8). There is an entrance here to a small car park which is round the back of the building.

HISTORY:
The Gospel Hall (or Meeting House) was the first of several Brethren Assemblies in Orkney and was built in 1869 on a piece of land bought from the Balfours of Shapinsay. It was built in response to another of Westray's schisms which saw an acrimonious secession of about two thirds of members from the Baptist Kirk. The hero or villain, depending on your perspective, was Price Hopkins, an enthusiastic young Baptist evangelist, who had theological leanings towards the Plymouth Brethren tradition. Henry Harcus in "The Orkney Baptists" charges Hopkins with covertly "undermining" Baptist principles for some time, though it should be noted that the book is written very much from the Baptist position and in an era when the wounds were still raw.

A small flat-roofed extension in 1974 saw kitchen and toilets added to the west end and this is where the main door is now, having once been at the east-facing gable end. The whole building was re-roofed in 1985 and a decade later the rest of the inside was refurbished.

Another decade on and the exterior was given a much-needed facelift, the building now looking pristine in its new white coat. The interior, in keeping with the Brethren Assembly tradition, is simple and unpretentious but well looked after.

COMMENT:

Inevitably it's been mentioned elsewhere in this booklet but it's important to note that those who led schism were not, for the most part, intent on disrupting things or causing any kind of hurt. They were people who believed staunchly in principles that were of great personal importance to them and they took their actions only after very careful and prayerful consideration, probably agonising in many cases.

All the current Westray congregations are born of dissent, including (and starting with) the Church of Scotland, which began in current form at the Scottish Reformation of 1560. Though division is today a source of regret for many Christians (rightly so in the view of this writer) it has also led to a diversity of style and opportunity that would not otherwise have happened. From this has evolved many small but faithful congregations who have nurtured the personal faith of many.

REFLECTION:

Meeting House followers have a long tradition of breaking and sharing bread every Sunday, something which has been sadly lost from many other Protestant Churches.

Lord Jesus,

You broke bread with those who were despised,
You shared wine with those who were frowned upon,
You called the poorest of the poor
And the weakest of the weak
To sit at your table in the Kingdom of God.

Called from the highways and the gutter,
You bring us, who are not fit to gather the crumbs from under
your table,
Into the upside-down wealth of your Kingdom
And to receive you in sacrament.

Thank you, is so utterly inadequate.
But thank you, all the same.

Amen.

Services every Sunday at 11.30am and 7pm

OLD KIRKHOUSE

HY 489 452

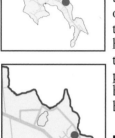

DIRECTIONS:

You'll see a sign for Miller's shop on the B9066 about three and a half miles north of Rapness Pier. Take this turning and follow the road over the brae until you reach the shore, where the road branches right to the shop or left (NW) towards the Bay of Swartmill. Just 50 yards or so on from here and the road cuts through a bit of higher banking retained by a wall on the left hand side. This is the site of Old Kirkhouse, though you'll have to negotiate the wall and fence if you're going in. There's a large passing place here as the road turns towards the shoreside again but as we're not supposed to park in passing places you may be better leaving a car back nearer the shop!

HISTORY:

This is one of our least obvious sites as the precise location of the Kirk is unknown but it's well worthy of inclusion because all the signs point to a significant enough building. Local tradition has long spoken of this as a lost chapel site and the place names in the area give weight to this.

The mound that the road now cuts through (recorded in some places as the "Mound of Skelwick") is the former farm settlement of Old Kirkhouse and reveals several bits of masonry, whilst a further quarter of a mile or so to the NW there are traces of the farm which was called the Manse and where a find of old coins was made many years ago. The present day farm of Kirkhouse overlooks the site from the south and older rental records refer to the farm names of Netherkirk and Overkirk.

There is little doubt that the area around the bay would once have been much more populous and all the evidence points to a late medieval (perhaps 13th century) chapel with the probability of an adjacent cemetery. The mound itself is about 45 yards in diameter and has revealed substantial archaeological deposits dating from this period. But the most likely site for the chapel structure appears to be in the small field immediately to the west of the enclosure which surrounds the mound.

COMMENT:
It's exciting to think what could lie just a few inches beneath the surface here, tantalisingly close yet inaccessible unless a proper excavation is ever organised. Westray and Papay (like the rest of Orkney) are packed with ancient remains just waiting either to be unveiled and rediscovered or to be destroyed forever by erosion or by human intervention.

There are quite literally hundreds of uninvestigated locations where a few stones or a small mound of some description appear far too organised or uniformly shaped to be a natural occurrence.

People are remarkably similar. What's seen on the surface often hides substantial things underneath, good or bad – good *and* bad, if we're honest.

There are people who think that living here must be like staying in some kind of island idyll. They have a distorted image which seems to be informed by a broth of sources from "Brigadoon" and "The Good Life" to "Katie Morag"! Living here can indeed be wonderful. But scratch just a little below the surface and you'll find people with the same hurts and wounds as anywhere else. Issues like grief, addiction, illness, loneliness, debt, depression, guilt etc. don't disappear just because they're covered over wherever and whenever you live.

The bottom line is that all folk are porous and fragile, especially those who deny it.

REFLECTION:
We like to pretend we're okay, Lord,
Papering over cracks,
Denying the vulnerability,
Avoiding the need to deal with it.
But you see through all the flannel
Paring back the edifice
Stripping away the veneer of wholeness
And exposing us for what we truly are ...

... loved by you
However broken we're revealed to be.

Amen.

PETERKIRK

HY 499 400

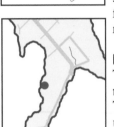

DIRECTIONS:

Leaving the Rapness ferry terminal turn left instead of heading right towards Pierowall. About ½ mile along this road you'll find a turn off to the right which heads up a low hill. About 100 yards on from here the road appears to end at the farm of Rusland but you'll see a track which veers slightly rightwards. Follow this down to the house of Stancro (end of the road!) and walk the 50 or so yards to the shore. Follow the shore to the left (SW) for another 50 – 100 yards and you'll arrive at the substantial mound that is the Peterkirk site.

HISTORY:

There are many Peterkirks (Chapels dedicated to St. Peter) throughout Orkney and other areas dominated by Norse culture. This one, like so many of the others appears to have been built upon a former Broch site.

There's not much to see above the surface today – a few traces of walling, several upright stones that clearly aren't here by accident and around the mound there are traces of what may have been buildings. It's obvious that much of the site has been lost to the sea whilst other masonry will have been plundered for later building projects, particularly the nearby walls.

Several archaeological investigations over the years have failed to find the exact location of the Chapel but a number of graves have been found and it's possible that the actual Kirk site has since been eroded by the sea. But the evidence supports its existence and it's quite likely that the Chapel would have pre-dated the Viking era (probably 8th century) and possibly continued through it.

COMMENT:

Like many of our featured sites, the Peterkirk sat next to the sea. If you look north from here over the Bay of Tuquoy you see the spine of hills that runs northwards and shelters the rest of the island from the worst of the Atlantic storms. Look west and you'll see the beautifully rugged isle of Rousay, wonderfully rich in its own ancient history. Look north west and you'll see the often wild Westray Firth and nothing else because beyond here the next stop is the southern tip of Greenland.

Like all island communities Westray and Papay have long had a dependency on the sea. More accurately we should say that they have an inter-dependency with the sea. For millennia it's been both the highway for communication and the source of a rich harvest. It's also been the recreational playground, a tradition continued today by the successful sailing club and ever-popular annual Westray Regatta (see *"Tight Sheets – Traditions and Tales"* by Westray Sailing Club).

But islanders the world over have always had a love-hate relationship with the sea and these two isles are no exception. Every moment of every day people here risk their lives fishing, crewing ferries, working as merchant seamen or serving in the oil industry's stand-by and supply vessels. At home others wait anxiously or raise disproportionately large funds for the RNLI. The sea brings life and the sea claims life. It is both a blessing and a curse.

REFLECTION:
"Oh, hear us when we cry to thee
For those in peril on the sea".
(William Whiting)

Turn your gaze seawards and think of those who are currently out there. Maybe a boat or two is visible but remember the many who are far out to sea, beyond our horizon but never beyond God's.

Those who go down to the sea in ships,
Who do business on great waters,
They see the works of the Lord,
And His wonders in the deep
(Psalm 107:23, 24 from NKJV)

Lord Jesus,
Calming waters
Stilling storms
Filling nets with a miraculous catch,
We remember those at sea just now
And those who wait at home
Yearning for the safe return of loved
ones.

Amen.

THE RAPNESS KIRKS

HY 494 426

DIRECTIONS:

About 1½ miles from the Rapness ferry terminal on the road heading north you'll pass both these buildings on the left-hand side just at a rightward bend in the road. They are very obviously former Churches and each sits beside a house which was formerly its Manse.

HISTORY:

We have two former Kirks here but with their history so intertwined they need to be taken together.

The smaller of the two Kirks was first used on 10th February 1878 by the Church of Scotland and its Manse was the adjacent bungalow (now known as The Dean). With regular attendances of 100 and more (including 80 communicant members) attempts were made in 1884 to place Rapness on the footing of independent parish status. This failed due to insufficient endowment.

The southernmost and larger of the two was completed in 1883, as home for the Free Church of Scotland congregation. The first service was held in April of that year and it was formally dedicated in July, services up till then having been held in the nearby schoolhouse (see page 34).

The Free Kirk building, which became UF (United Free) following the national union of 1900, was definitely the superior of the two, boasting pointed arched windows faced with red sandstone, a sloping floor and a unique air conditioning system. This involved ventilation flues being connected to ceiling vents, dormer vents in the roof and a pull-cord system to regulate the flow. Sadly, but perhaps typically with experimental technology, the new system was abandoned within a short time, possibly as a result of the fierce storm in January 1884, which caused some structural damage.

It's locally suggested that the two congregations had a "race" to be first to open the doors but records show that this is rather fanciful as there was a gap of over five years between the erection of the two buildings.

The Church of Scotland bought the UF Kirk and Manse in 1926 when the UF congregation was subsumed into their sister congregation in the north of the isle (see page 30). The bigger Kirk became the Church with the smaller becoming its hall. The Dean was sold and the UF Manse became the C of S Manse and eventually the Manse for the whole Parish …still with me?

The two Kirk buildings were last used in 1971 and were eventually sold to local farmers as stores. The original Free Kirk Manse remained as the island's C of S Manse until June 2003 when a new Manse at Hilldavale in the Dykeside district was purchased.

The status of the C of S building (and UF from 1900) was always one of a "Mission Station". In other words, the ordained "parish" Minister retained overall responsibility for ministerial matters but was often assisted by an en-situ and part-time "missionary" who would conduct most services and deal with pastoral matters within the mission area. The Mission Station took responsibility for many of its own affairs but came under the jurisdiction of the "parish" Kirk Session. The missionaries were usually unsalaried but received a small allowance as well as the house.

The need to maintain a separate congregation at Rapness diminished in part due to population decline. But it also reflected demographic changes that were mirrored in other services and facilities such as shops and schooling. Quite simply, over the years roads improved and private car ownership increased, making the bigger and better building further north much more accessible than it had once been.

COMMENT:
Now it seems anomalous to have two Kirk buildings built so close to each other. Today, the Baptist, UF and Church of Scotland congregations work together on a regular and wide variety of activities and services, respecting differences but recognising that there is far more to bind than to divide.

In 2003 the UF and Church of Scotland took this into a more formal partnership by signing a Covenant which promises increasing co-operation on a wide range of issues and offers repentance for allowing past issues to divide. The Covenant can be seen inside both the current buildings (see pages 12 & 30). Both congregations continue to work with their Baptist neighbours and to seek ways to serve the community together.

Any relationship, formal or informal, requires give as well as take, but the overwhelming response from the congregations has been that it is enriching to share our journey and that the Church is better at being the Church when it can be so together. There is still progress to make but days have changed. Thanks be to God.

REFLECTION:
One dark Friday
One Easter morning
One Risen Christ
One Holy Spirit
One body
One people
One hope
One choice
One way together.
Amen.

SHEEPIE KIRK

HY 445 468

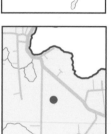

DIRECTIONS:

The Kirk stands a mile or so south of Pierowall virtually half way between the B9066 (Rapness to Pierowall) and the B9067 (Pierowall to Westside). The simplest way to get there is from the Westside Road, heading east for about 300 yards opposite the farm of Quoys but you'll need to negotiate fences and sometimes boggy ground. If there's livestock here you may need to come in another way. There's no designated parking space but there is a largish lay-by on the left hand (heading south) side of the road. Don't just park up on the verge or you may end up in a ditch!

HISTORY:

Despite the lack of easy access this is a quite substantial building and a visit is well worth the effort. Opened in 1823 as a United Presbyterian Kirk it must have seemed like a great luxury to the congregation who had been worshipping in the barn at Brough (see page 33).

With four walls still standing, the scale of the building is evident. It was built to seat 300 worshippers and a balcony ran the length of the north (windowless) wall. This was later extended round both ends, increasing the seating capacity to about 450. The four arched windows in the south wall are still in place and between the middle ones you can see the sockets where the towering pulpit stood. The east and west walls (both with doors) were gabled with the last one pulled down in 1952 after the other had blown down in a hurricane.

The drystane wall surrounding the whole property has deteriorated and traces of the old access road, which led directly north, are barely visible now.

Despite its considerable size the thriving congregation (who became UF in 1900 following a national union) were starting to outgrow it and the Church became surplus to use when the current UF Kirk (see page 30) was built in 1867. Thereafter it was simply abandoned to the sheep from where the present name comes.

The now ruined Session House abuts the north wall and was a dwelling house until well into the 20th century.

COMMENT:

It looks deceptively small from some angles but once inside the scale is impressive. On a prominent hilltop site, this was one of the biggest buildings in Westray and you can guarantee it could have been built only through considerable effort and generous giving. It's all the more remarkable then, that the whole building was abandoned just 44 years later, especially when you consider that another monumental effort was required to create the new building, which stands only quarter of a mile away.

To critics it may have seemed profligate but to others it was a remarkable step of faith – a determination that when it came to giving God his due, second best could not be tolerated. There must also have been a great sense of optimism and a spirit of growth as the historic decision to move on was made.

We really shouldn't be surprised because throughout the nation the United Presbyterian Church had by this time developed a reputation for forward thinking and radical action. This was seen clearly in things such as worship style, progressive social and political concerns (especially inclusive education, care of the poor and a determined opposition to privilege). Why should it be any surprise that well maintained modern buildings were also high on the agenda?

REFLECTION:
Leaving the familiar behind (even when it's comparatively new) is never an easy step. It appears that our natural tendency is to cling to those things which re-enforce our comfort or our sense of security. Jesus warned against this.

Lord Jesus,
Make us vibrant,
Receptive to your call,
Meeting your challenge to change
and to keep changing

.......effervescent wine
poured into new skins
semper reformanda
Amen.

ST. MARY'S

HY 439 488

DIRECTIONS:

Just north of Pierowall village, heading for Gill Pier, you'll find the substantial ruin of St. Mary's (or Lady Kirk) right on the shore. Enter by the cemetery gates, where there is car parking space and you'll see the now roofless building down to your right.

HISTORY:

It's widely believed that a Church building of some description stood here since the early 12th century. Indeed, the Orkneyinga Saga makes reference to such a building in 1136, telling us that none less than Earl Rognvald attended worship there, during his campaign to subjugate local leaders and claim the Earldom.

Of the current structure, the earliest parts (primarily the south wall of the nave) appear to date from the 13th century, with substantial rebuilding in 1674. Two impressive gravestones from this period have been rescued from weathering and are protected behind glass screens in the chancel.

St. Mary's was last used as a Parish Church in 1879 and fell into disrepair thereafter. Now roofless, the main walls are largely intact and a complete arch still spans the border between chancel and nave.

You can't approach St. Mary's without first walking through the substantial burial ground that surrounds it. The new cemetery to the north is separated from the old by a wall with the main gate on the roadside and a smaller opening between the two to the south west of the dividing wall.

The building is maintained in its current state by Historic Scotland.

COMMENT:

Whilst the Kirk building is justifiably one of Westray's main visitor attractions, the surrounding cemetery is a key part of the whole setting. Note how the stones in the older part sit in tight rows with all the inscriptions facing the sea. As you get closer to the Kirk you'll come across the very old stones, standing upright in the uneven ground. Those going back many centuries now have illegible inscriptions, erased by the effects of weathering. Indeed it's remarkable that so many have survived at all in such an exposed location. The oldest burials to the immediate south of the Kirk entrance are marked by low flag stones, some little more than stumps, but still standing as sentinel markers.

For several years now, worshippers from different congregations have gathered here in the early hours of Easter Day to herald the Resurrection morning together. It's the perfect setting for such an event, for not only do the old walls provide some shelter, but there's something wonderful about the experience of them echoing again to the ringing of praise as they've done for nearly a millennium ... and all of this surrounded by the visible memorials of those who have gone before us in this faith and who are already Risen because of Easter Day.

REFLECTION:

It's not difficult to imagine how the building would have looked when it was a regular place of worship and there's a powerful poignancy added by the surrounding burial ground. Stand inside the Kirk and look at the ancient walls. Close your eyes and listen in your head to the early Latin chants or later Scots Psalms being offered to God, listen to the wind, to the sea.

Gracious God,
Many generations of your people have been Baptised here,
Worshipped here,
Learned of you here,
Lie buried here.

We give thanks for all those who have gone before us and shaped our lives:
Those known by name,
And those who are no longer even distant memories to us,
But who are forever known personally to you:
Those whose lives are not ended,
But eternal
In both quality and quantity.

Make us worthy of this legacy.
Amen.

There are records of gravestone inscriptions at the Heritage Centre archive.

UNITED FREE CHURCH

HY 445 473

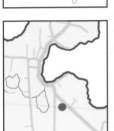

DIRECTIONS:

Like its Parish Kirk neighbour (see page 12) one mile to the south, the UF building (known locally as the New Kirk) sits prominently astride a hill top. You'll find it on the left hand side (heading north) on the B9066 towards Pierowall. The old building (gable end on to the road) is distinctly ecclesiastical in shape and is unmistakably a Church. Turn left immediately before it and you'll find ample parking space. The hall to the rear is the space currently in use by the congregation. The building is usually locked but visits can be pre-arranged through the minister, whose Manse is at the top of the car park.

HISTORY:

Built to replace the earlier Sheepie Kirk (see page 26) the UP (later UF) Kirk became the largest in the island when opened in May 1867. The adjoining hall was dedicated to the memory of Rev. George Reid who died in 1862 and was minister of the congregation during the Sheepie Kirk years of 1823 – 1861. It was completed in 1899 and a painting of the same Rev. Reid (an enthusiastic promoter of all things educational) along with a commemorative plaque can be found on the north wall of the hall which still bears his name. The Manse, which sits just above the hall, was actually the first building on the site, being completed in 1862.

The large Kirk itself was a magnificent building inside and though it now has a rather derelict look, there's still enough to show the splendour it once held. The large central pulpit, fenced table, and choir stalls have a grand, almost judicial, air to them and the rest of the Kirk (substantial balcony on three sides) has fixed rows with pew doors throughout.

The congregation moved out in 1980 and services are now held in the quite homely Reid Memorial Hall, which had been in use for services during the winter months for several years previously.

COMMENT:
Like all disused buildings in this part of the world it hasn't taken long for decay to set into the large Kirk and the interior has become musty and shabby. But to stand inside the large building today remains an evocative experience. All disused places of worship generate this feeling to some extent but this one particularly so as little has changed, other than general decline to the fabric and fittings. Indeed it would be an unimaginatively dull person who couldn't visualise this packed Kirk and perhaps even hear them raising the rafters with Psalms.

The "New Kirk" label has stuck from the days when the congregation seceded from the then "established Kirk" (or Old Kirk), firstly as United Presbyterians, then United Free. To do so was a huge step, cutting across family ties and traditions going back many generations but these were people of great conviction and no small faith, people who didn't dissent lightly but who stood on firm principle and who were prepared to take the risk for something they believed strongly in.

Though the original issues of secession have long since been resolved, the faith and resilience of these reluctant revolutionaries must never be forgotten.

REFLECTION:
Lord, make us into people who are
prepared to take risks for you,
To do what we know to be right
And to go where you call us to
Even when such movement challenges
our complacency
And threatens our perceived security.

Thank you for those whose lives continue
to inspire us:
People who choose to stride out with you
Rather than sit in their comfort zone.

Help us to raise our own discipleship to
such levels.

Amen.

Services at 11.30 am every Sunday.
Evening services variable.

Westray Straw

Straw-back chairs made in Westray in the time-honoured way, using black oat straw, white oak and sea grass. An ancient Westray craft still being practised today.

Contact: **Edith Costie**
           01857 677411
           edith.costie@btinternet.com
           www.westraystudios.co.uk

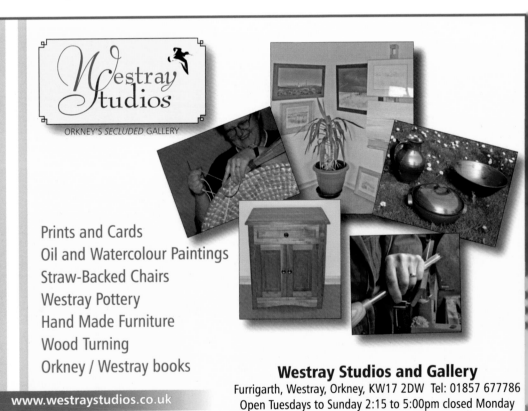

Westray Studios
ORKNEY'S *SECLUDED* GALLERY

Prints and Cards
Oil and Watercolour Paintings
Straw-Backed Chairs
Westray Pottery
Hand Made Furniture
Wood Turning
Orkney / Westray books

www.westraystudios.co.uk

Westray Studios and Gallery
Furrigarth, Westray, Orkney, KW17 2DW Tel: 01857 677786
Open Tuesdays to Sunday 2:15 to 5:00pm closed Monday

WESTRAY HOUSES

There are several houses in Westray which at one time or another were important places of worship. It's stating the obvious, but if currently inhabited, any visit will have to be by arrangement and at the owner's discretion. For similar reasons no attempt is being made here to give much in the way of contemporary description but it's important to note the vital role that these places have played in Westray's ecclesiastical history. It has therefore been decided to include them all, whether currently inhabited or empty, in this single section.

THE VESTRAY (tucked in behind Fiold and overlooking Rackwick and Aikerness) was built as both a Chapel and manse for the Congregational Church who were formed in 1803. The building was completed in August 1804 and became the Baptist Chapel (known then as the Tabernacle) in 1810 when the congregation changed allegiance from the Congregationalist to Baptist tradition. Vestry remained in use as a place of worship until the dedication of the new Baptist Kirk in 1850 (see page 8) since when it has been a private house and is still inhabited as such.

Further south stands another current dwelling house that was once a Baptist Kirk. EAST CHAPEL, sits at an unusual angle hard onto the main road, a few hundred yards south of the Parish Kirk (just opposite the old road which runs in a straight line to Cleaton House). It was built in 1839 and served Baptists in the south of the isle. It appears to have ceased as a chapel following the 1850 opening of the new Baptist Kirk.

The farmhouse of BROUGH remains one of Westray's most imposing buildings, despite rapidly falling into dilapidation. It's almost opposite the UF Kirk, a couple of hundred yards to the east, and now stands without most of its roof. Brough, or to be precise, the large barn in its steading, was the home of the UP congregation from its formation in 1821 until the opening of the Sheepie Kirk (see page 26) in 1823.

NOLTLAND CASTLE (1/2 mile west of Pierowall on the road to Noup Head) played a similar temporary role but to the Congregational (later Baptist) congregation from the spring of 1803 until late summer 1804. The congregation met in the large barrel-vaulted hall and kitchen on the ground floor, which they called Noltland Hall. Despite their best efforts to make it homely it was dark, damp and must have been bitterly cold in the winter. Much has been written elsewhere about the castle (it must be the most recorded building in the isle). Suffice to note for this purpose that it was the regular site for a worshipping congregation at least once and possibly twice (see page 54). The castle is maintained by Historic Scotland and is open to the public. The key hangs by the back door of Noltland farm (opposite the main gate).

There are several "OLD SCHOOL"s dotted around Westray. The one in Rapness is now a family home as well as being the base of the island's largest building contractor, Daniel Harcus Construction, who have themselves worked on many of the buildings and sites listed in these pages. The original classroom (at what's now the office end of the building) was a regular place of worship for two or three years,

used by Westray's only Free Kirk congregation until the building of the Kirk (see page 24) in 1878. It's not known exactly when the congregation started meeting in the Old School but likely dates are from 1875 or 1876, although there are suggestions that they met here for some years prior to that. This is quite possible although it was August 1876 when they were formally constituted as a congregation of the Free Church of Scotland.

TRENABIE MILL sits on the south side of Pierowall, a little way off the main road. It's an imposing building which has been lovingly restored as a family home in recent years by Willie and Sandy McEwen. Westray's highest "greenhouse" sits in the glass roof above the kiln, a roof which covers what is effectively a three-storey atrium. It's also one of Westray's least likely and less well known places of worship. Sandy and Willie are Quakers (Society of Friends) and Friends Meetings are held here most Sunday mornings at 9.30am. When the Mill is otherwise let out to guests the meetings are held at the family home of the old Westside Manse (contact the McEwens for details).

There is some speculation as to whether or not there was ever a chapel at the BU and, if so, where it was sited. Several archaeological surveys refer to it with Sarah Jane Gibbon's (as yet unpublished) thesis suggesting that the real site may be near the present day Rapness cemetery, which itself was quite possibly on the site of

an older burial ground. It is however, very likely that a house of such significance since at least the Viking era would have contained a chapel (probably for family use) within its walls. Although the current house dates from just 1897, the Bu has long been a high status residence and in Norse times would have been the most significant farm in the area. The remains of the previous house are visible in the ground immediately in front of the current building.

Of particular interest is Alison Gray's suggestion in "Circle of Light" that the Chapel at the Bu may well have been the scene of the last Latin Mass in Orkney following the Protestant Reformation of 1560.

If that is indeed the case then it was almost certainly the last Catholic Mass celebrated in Westray until 1970, when Fr. Bertie Bamber SJ celebrated Mass at NORTH COTTOHOWAN. Catholic Mass has subsequently been celebrated in 1991 at the OLD SCHOOL, Skelwick (again by Fr. Bamber) and in 2003 at HAVELSEY COTTAGE, Pierowall (home of Michael Blair) by Fr. Gerard Hassey SJ.

A small group described as "Exclusive Brethren" are reported to have met somewhere at BRECKOWALL (on the western edge of Pierowall) in the late 19th and early 20th century, although there's some doubt as to which of the houses they met in. In fact, evidence for their existence amounts to little more that a couple of second-hand recollections and when and why they came to cease as a worshipping group is unknown.

HEATHERVIEW, originally a workers' bothy in the same farm, is said to have been a Good Templars' meeting place. The Good Templars were staunchly evangelical and vehemently prohibitionist concerning alcohol. They reached their peak in the late 19th / early 20th century with over 1,300 branches (known as lodges) throughout Scotland, including Orkney. It is quite possible that both these organisations had some overlap.

Now little more than a shed above Duniro (on Coastguards hill immediately south of Pierowall), CLAYBRAES was once the island's fast-food epicentre. Originally a private house, it operated as the chippy from 1961 to 1977 and for a few years during the late '60s and early '70s it was also the centre for fortnightly "Gospel meetings" on Sunday evenings with music provided by the "chippy band". The meetings were organised primarily by local Baptists and the age group was predominantly that of older teenagers and young adults, with sometimes up to fifty folk attending.

Westray Processors

SUPPLIERS OF QUALITY CRAB MEAT

GILL PIER
WESTRAY
ORKNEY
KW17 2DL
Tel 01857 677273

GOSPEL HALL

HY 495 535

DIRECTIONS:
The Hall is located between the houses of North Haven and Whitelooms towards the north end of Papay. It's small, rectangular and could easily pass for a domestic garage or shed but for the notice board on the wall which identifies it. It's easy to find, just off the main road on the right hand side if heading north and about 100 yards beyond Rose Cottage, which itself is painted pink and is unmissable! There is plenty room for cars to park.

HISTORY:
It seems that preachers from the Brethren tradition first started visiting Papay in the early part of the 20th century and they were obviously well enough received or they wouldn't have kept coming back. The first recorded Baptisms were in 1933.

For some years thereafter the congregation met in barns at Kimbland and Nistaben (where the barn was designed specially to hold meetings) and also in the house at Stripes. Indeed for many years meetings were held in Stripes for two Sundays running, followed by Nistaben on the third Sunday. This arrangement meant that a presence was maintained in both the north and south ends of the isle.

Throughout much of that time many people attended the meetings as well as attending services in the Parish Kirk. There appears to have been much more overlap between the two denominations than is usual today where local loyalties seem more likely to be with one or the other. It was, for example, quite common to sing in the choir at the Kirk service in the morning and then attend the Brethren meeting in the evening, or for children from Parish Kirk families to regularly attend the Brethren-run Sunday School.

A change of ownership at Stripes led to a change of venue and the Papay school was used for some time until the building of the current Gospel Hall in 1975, erected by the congregation with assistance from friends who came from Westray and further afield to lend a hand.

The whole building, comprising the meeting room and little else other than toilets, is unpretentious and unadorned. The exterior is plain with harled walls. The interior is equally modest but dignified with the grey chairs and cream walls being only slightly offset by a splash of colour from the pink curtains.

COMMENT:

One of the defining characteristics of Brethren Assemblies is their reluctance to become too reliant upon salaried or full-time clergy. It's true that a small number of assemblies employ a pastor / preacher but they're all much further south, much larger and they're certainly in the minority. The overwhelming majority of congregations within the Brethren tradition have rejected such a course.

There's not enough space here to do justice to any serious debate about the merits or demerits of full-time ministry but is it not the case that, in those Churches who do pay a stipend, there is a huge danger that the minister is left to deal with everything and the empowerment of God's people is consequently stifled?

To do so is not only foolish, but can also be regarded as sinful as we have no right to attempt to hold back the work of the Holy Spirit and her empowering gifts. God calls all his followers into service and ministry of some form. Our personal task therefore becomes one of discernment rather than denial.

Unleashing the full potential of all God's people should be a top priority within all Churches.

REFLECTION:

A few loaves,
A couple of small fish,
We've so little to give
Yet so much when given
in faith.

Empower your people, Lord,
And set your Church free
from all that is elitist.
Amen.

KIRK O' HOWE

HY 493 531

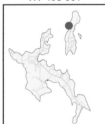

DIRECTIONS:

Go north past the turn-off for St. Boniface (see page 44) for about 300 yards and you'll find the Kirk site on the left hand side of the road, just before the private road to the house of Quoys. There are no obvious buildings, just a large uneven mound, of which the east side is actually cut through by the main road.

HISTORY:

There's a quite sizeable mound here (about 3m high and almost 90m in diameter) and it's quite probable that it could contain the remains of various other buildings as well – a farm steading, perhaps – one source even speaks of a "broch type structure".

There are no signs on the surface today of anything that could be readily identified as a place of worship but there's plenty other evidence for its existence. Various older surveys and records refer to a "religious house" the "Kirk o Hoo" and even a "popish chapel", complete with burial ground, being either on the site of the present mound or very close to it. Local tradition speaks of it as having doors on the south, west and north walls with divorcees having to use different doors! It's said that the west door was the main door and after the annulment ceremony, the woman left by the north and the man by the south.

It can be fairly surmised that it was a pre-reformation building and is likely to have been disused from the 1560 Reformation or earlier. Being in such close proximity to St. Boniface Kirk is not a great surprise as it's not uncommon for a Church with a more pastoral remit (or indeed a private chapel) to be in the same community as a monastery and it's quite probable that Boniface was a monastic settlement prior to its post-Reformation Parish role. It's been suggested that the building stone was quarried from the Bay of Burland on Papay's east coast.

COMMENT:

It's disconcerting how something which meant so much to the lives of people can now be almost without trace. This is especially so when part of the site appears to have been a burial ground. We wonder why sites of such importance were abandoned and eventually destroyed by our ancestors. It seems insensitive, even disrespectful. Yet the process of moving on and rebuilding (and often re-using the same material) is still very much in practice today.

REFLECTION:

Loving Father,

We are but visitors,
Transient,
Passing through,
While all else is in change.

This instability is unsettling
It injures our pride
When we realise how infinitesimally small we are
In the wider scale of things

Yet we are never insignificant
Because your stamp of love is upon us
You have called us by name
And your love is both personal and eternal.

Give us the wisdom to store our treasures in you
And forever.

Amen.

ST. ANN'S

HY 494 515

DIRECTIONS:

St. Ann's is easy to find – a comparatively large whitewashed building in the centre of Papay, next to the Community School, and a couple of hundred yards down hill from the Guest House and shop. The Kirk abuts the road and parking is available beside the football pitch opposite the front door.

HISTORY:

It was in 1842 that the Papay Laird, Thomas Traill began the building of a new Parish Kirk to replace the ageing St. Boniface (see page 44) but the doors were not yet open when "the Disruption"

split the then Church of Scotland in two. Traill bucked the national trend of the landed classes by supporting the Secession and taking most of the Papay congregation with him into the Free Church. In 1844, his sister, Ann Traill, formally gifted the building to the Free Church, the first in the country to be given over in this way. Ann died shortly afterwards, aged just 24, and the unusual dedication is in honour of her.

Major alterations in 1868 saw the removal of the balcony, and the traditional box pews were replaced by the more fashionable west-facing rows.

When the Church of Scotland and (by then) United Free Church came back together in 1929, St. Ann's became the Parish Kirk of the newly united congregation.

Over following decades the population dwindled and St. Ann's became underused and unsuited for the needs of a modern congregation. Fabric deteriorated and the dampness problem became chronic. This was addressed by a major renovation in 2000/2001 when a partnership of Church, Health Board and Council saw the building redeveloped as a flexible worship space, community facility and surgery. It also houses a self-contained flat, used primarily by student ministers and relief

nurses, a pattern which has now been copied elsewhere.

A free leaflet explaining more about the history and the renovation is available in St. Ann's.

THE BUILDING IS ALWAYS OPEN AND VISITORS ARE WELCOME AT ANY TIME.
PUBLIC WORSHIP – EVERY SUNDAY AT 2.30pm.

COMMENT:

By the 1990s St. Ann's stood as a symbol of neglect and decay, home to a congregation that didn't have the required resources to restore it. Now, since the congregation have turned that round, it stands as a symbol of renewal and of hope and has restored the Kirk to the very centre of the community – a facility where spiritual, social and health care needs are met in a unique partnership.

The surgery is the only part of the building which is not designed to be multi-purpose. All other areas have fully flexible fittings, with the sanctuary and community room being separated by a moveable partition so that a much larger space can be created. The pulpit dates from 1866 but was considerably scaled down during the recent alterations.

There are two beautiful felt banners on the south wall, based on the words of Psalm 104. Locally designed and made, they speak loudly of the links between the Kirk and the wider community it serves. Amongst several items produced by the local children is a wonderful banner on the north wall depicting a montage of wild birds. Also impressive is the mural on the outside of the west wall. It was made in 2004 using stones, shells and other items gathered from local beaches.

REFLECTION:

Look at the banner interpretations of Psalm 104 and pause to think about God as Creator and re-Creator. In a place like Papay the sights, sounds and smells of creation are never distant. They constantly surround us and call us to attune ourselves to them. This cycle of life and death, on land and in sea, is a constant reminder of something Otherly and Spiritual, something wonderful yet accessible, something infinite yet close enough to touch.

Loving Lord,
We praise you for renewal ...
- *of community*
- *of relationship*
- *of Church*
- *of life*
- *of hope*

and we thank you that despite our best efforts to damage this fragile world, its beauty and wonder is still here to inspire us and demand better of us as we catch glimpses of you within.

Amen.

ST. BONIFACE KIRK

HY 488 526

DIRECTIONS:
The Kirk and burial ground lie almost halfway along Papay's western shore. You can walk along the coast from the wonderfully evocative setting of the Knap of Howar (at almost 4000 BC, the oldest house in Northern Europe). Just head north for 10 – 15 minutes and use the stiles to the north side of the Kirk. By car, turn left about half a mile north of the airfield (it's signposted) and you'll find the car park a further quarter of a mile or so down the track and right by the Kirk gate.

HISTORY:
The first Church on this site, probably a wooden structure, and almost certainly part of a much larger monastic community, has been dated to the 8th century. It was the dominant Church centre (and likely the Bishopric seat) for all of Orkney and possibly for substantially further afield.

The oldest parts of the current building date to the 12th century but most of what we can see is later. An extensive refit took place in the early 18th century, with the chancel removed from the east side and a balcony with outside stair added to the west. The interior was fitted with box pews and a high central pulpit fixed to the south wall.

Thereafter St. Boniface served as the parish Kirk but lost most of its members to the Free Kirk following the Disruption of 1843 and opening of St. Ann's in 1844 (see page 42). In 1929, following the reunion of the United Free Church and Church of Scotland, St. Ann's (by then UF) became the building of choice and Boniface fell into decline. By the late 1980s most of the interior was beyond repair, the roof was collapsing and it was in danger of becoming ruinous.

That we're now able to report on a wonderfully restored building rather than a pile of stones is huge tribute to the community effort that resulted in a loving restoration and the rededication of the Kirk in June 1994.

The surrounding cemetery has some fascinating headstones, most notably the famous hogback stone, to the east of the Kirk.

COMMENT:
A strange place to site an important Kirk?

In many ancient sites what lies beneath the ground is far more extensive than what is now visible. This is certainly the case here. Don't be fooled by its apparent isolation. St. Boniface stands upon a substantial settlement site, with an Iron Age broch and many other buildings spreading out over fully ten acres and going back to at least the 7th century BC, possibly well beyond.

All the evidence points to continuous habitation of this place for well over a thousand years before the Kirk was built. The presence of the broch further implies that it was a place of some prestige and power.

Remember also that in an era when virtually all travel was by sea, Papay was ideally situated as a missionary and administrative base for the whole of both Orkney and Shetland.

So forget the idea of a Kirk at the edge – this was a Kirk in the midst:
- It was in the centre of a market place for trade and commerce.
- It was at the heart of a major travel interchange.
- It was where authority was wielded and justice administered.
- It was in the High Street of life, where people lived, worked and died.

It was exactly where the Church must be.

REFLECTION:
God in the midst
Your way is not to skirt round the edges
Or to major on trivia.

Forgive our obsession with peripheral issues
Arranging, administering, prettifying
Polishing the champagne flutes as folk thirst
Folding our napkins as they starve.

May your Church, Lord,
stand with you and your people
never hidden away
- a Church in the midst
serving her Lord in the midst.

Amen.

An excellent little guide book ("St. Boniface Kirk") is available in the Kirk priced £2

SERVICES ON OCCASIONAL BASIS – SEE LOCAL NOTICES.

ST. TREDWELL'S

HY 496 508

DIRECTIONS:
The walk to St. Tredwell's is pleasant enough but is definitely "cross-country", with the Chapel sitting on the east shore of the Loch and about a mile or so from the nearest road. You can approach from the south, heading north from the Bay of Bothican or from the north via the old mill at Hookin. The distance is similar. The lochside can be quite marshy and boggy so it's best to take the higher paths and wellies are advisable. There are a few fences and walls to get over but most have good stiles to assist.

HISTORY:
St. Tredwell's was once a major pilgrimage site and evidence shows that pilgrims, particularly those with eyesight problems came from throughout Orkney and well beyond to seek healing. St. Tredwell herself (also known as Triduana) is said to have plucked out her own eyes and skewered them on a thorn in a rather dramatic gesture to show she had eyes only for God and thus, to spurn the advances of Nechtan, King of the Picts.

The Chapel almost certainly stood upon an earlier Iron Age complex, possibly a broch and the (previously island) setting suggests that it may once even have been a crannog.

This is a site that's positively crying out to reveal its secrets. All the little traces of walling, the mounds and ditches, even glimpses of tunnel, suggest that something very substantial once stood here. Now with all these layers lying partially collapsed and on top of one another it's difficult for the untrained eye to make any sense of it but there's more than enough to make it all feel tantalisingly close.

Various artefacts including a stone ball have been recovered and can be found at the National Museum of Antiquities in Edinburgh and Tankerness House Museum in Kirkwall.

COMMENT:

At first glance this appears to be little more than a pile of rubble atop an exposed promontory but in reality it was once a site of prime importance and a place by which people laid great hope. It's a strange thought today that hundreds of people should travel vast distances in an era when travel was long and hazardous just to reach this spot. To achieve such a reputation some spectacular miracles must have been attributed to the intervention of St. Tredwell, who is said to have been buried beneath the Chapel.

Many of us today, baulk at the thought of such saintly veneration and devotion to the cult of a human being, however pious or faithful that person may have been. But we mustn't lose sight of the fact that this was a place of innate hope and resonant faith.

People came with a belief and confidence that God's healing power was more accessible in places like this because of the saint's spiritual presence. The sacrifice and effort made to get here must have been very considerable for some. But still they came and continued to come even after the Reformation was supposed to have swept such "superstition" away.

But that's the power of hope and hope was embedded here.

REFLECTION:

Sit down and look out to the loch. Pilgrims are said to have circumnavigated it, often several times, on their knees as a show of penitence. Remember that many of these folk had serious eyesight problems, even blindness. But they came in faith to seek healing.

Christ the healer,
Who brought sight to the blind,
Mobility to the lame,
Cure to the leper,
Hope to the neglected
Even life to the dead.

Hear our prayer for those who long to know that healing today And give us the faith to share in that process By offering our love and support in all ways, always.

Amen.

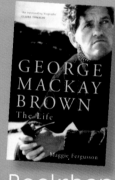

COMMUNITY BUILDINGS

Attached to the north east side of PIEROWALL SCHOOL in the heart of the village, the COMMUNITY HALL and COMMUNITY ROOM were opened in 1988 and though well used for many events there's little about them that could be described as attractive. Both lack natural light, have a very basic, utilitarian feel to them and as essential buildings for school as well as community have had their aesthetic integrity compromised over the

years. The Community Room especially, looks more like a store room some times. Nevertheless these spaces, particularly the Community Room (and on occasion the Hall) were used as a regular place of worship until very recently.

From the early 1990s until late 2003, a monthly "Fellowship Meeting" met here (as a "neutral" venue) on Sunday evenings. The meetings were supported by the Baptist, Church of Scotland and UF congregations and were largely praise based with a high musical content, drawing on the talents of local (and occasionally visiting) musicians. The meetings often had a speaker to address them and always concluded with a shared cuppa.

Even towards the end, the Fellowship Meetings often had fifty or more in attendance but the organisers made a conscious and brave decision to stop them as it was felt that many of the original purposes (eg. bringing the different congregations together, introducing new hymns etc.) were now being met by the weekly united evening services, something that didn't exist when the meetings began.

Though never a separate denomination, the Fellowship Meetings are a significant part of Westray's recent Church history. They did much in bringing worshippers from different traditions together and normalising the idea of united worship.

The Community Room is also the venue for a weekly assembly/service (Wednesdays at noon), in which Primary School children gather to sing hymns and reflect on a topical issue, often with input from one of the local ministers and sometimes organised by the classes to reflect current project work. Longer Secondary assemblies are held several times a year and are usually in the Community Classroom (or Art Room) by the school's front door.

Over the years, the Community Hall and Room have been used for one-off events including Church services and in recent years the school's Christmas Carol Service (held on the last day of the Christmas term) has established itself as a community-wide event of some significance.

PAPAY COMMUNITY SCHOOL, right next to St. Ann's has also seen multi-purpose use over the years but became a regular Sunday Church venue as home to the Church of Scotland congregation from August 2000 until April 2001 when St. Ann's was closed for major renovations. School pupils and staff went out of their way to accommodate the congregation, who were delighted to return the favour a year or two later, with the school making use of Kirk facilities, particularly for PE and dining room, due to refurbishment work. The school was also used as a meeting place prior to the building of the Gospel Hall in 1975 (see page 38).

The part of the school used by the congregation is on the roadside of the building and is now the community hall, though at the time it was used for all school activities, including the classroom.

The **KALISGARTH** facility in Westray opened in 2005, after a number of years of community planning and lobbying, initiated by Westray Development Trust. Run by Orkney Islands Council it provides much-needed residential and day-care facilities within the isle. The building is towards the north end of Pierowall and is reached by road through Howanbrek (beside Rendall's shop, opposite Tulloch's). It features the same part-piended roof shape as both the Parish and Baptist Kirks and was designed by Kirkwall based Leslie Burgher, whose father, George, is a Westray man. A special feature is the wonderful window, designed and made by local youngsters under the watchful guidance of stained-glass artist, Fiona Foley.

It was agreed at an early stage that Kalisgarth should become the venue for regular united services and after some discussion in was decided to hold these every two months on a Sunday evening. They are jointly hosted by the Baptist, Church of Scotland and UF congregations, start at 7pm and last for just 30 minutes, followed by the obligatory Westray cuppa. At the first such service, held on 6th November 2005, the three congregations presented a locally made table-top lectern and large-print Bible to "the Kalisgarth community". The frequency of services here will be reviewed and may yet increase.

War memorials are hardly buildings but they are community monuments and are also the scene of regular annual (and sometimes more frequent) worship. The **WESTRAY WAR MEMORIAL** is just past the cemetery, heading north out of Pierowall and on the opposite side of the road. A short act of Remembrance is held every Remembrance Day (usually 10.55am for about 10 minutes). It is supported by folk of all Kirks and none and is traditionally led by the ministers. A two minute silence is observed and a wreath is laid by one of Westray's ex-servicemen. Remembrance Day services are then held in the respective Kirks with a united service in the evening. Other acts of Remembrance have been held here from time to time, by visiting groups of ex-servicemen, most notably the RAF Association of Orkney.

The **PAPAY WAR MEMORIAL** is halfway between Holland Farm and the airfield, on the east side of the road. The annual Remembrance Day service here takes place around 3.30pm following the Parish Kirk service, which itself begins at 2.30pm. The format is similar to that described for Westray. Both the Papay and Westray war memorials are fairly typical single needle monuments set in small roadside recesses.

The Good Templars (see page 36) also held meetings in St. George's Hall, which is now the **WESTRAY HERITAGE CENTRE**. This building is tucked in behind the Pierowall Hotel in the centre of the village and has seen many uses over the years. It was originally a school, founded by Rev. George Reid (see page 30) in 1853 and has served, amongst other things, as a village hall, RAF billet, Home Guard base and Army Cadet HQ. As the Heritage Centre it is a huge asset to the island and is a "must do" for any visitor, housing some excellent displays and a wonderful archive which covers many of the sites featured in this book. There is also a small café and shop selling local crafts and heritage related items. Over the years, it has been used for various Church services and special events, including being the base for the celebrated "Tell Scotland" mission led by D P Thomson throughout July and August 1956, during which many services were held here.

UNCERTAIN SITES

Many of the sites mentioned in these pages have *some* uncertainty about them but there are a few which have little to support their claim other than very sketchy evidence or local tradition alone. These things, of course, change as new evidence is (quite literally) unearthed but for the time being we'll simply note them here and put them on an appropriate shelf.

VIA (there are two buildings that currently bear the name – North Via and South Via) sits on Papay's eastern shore at the bay of North Wick. There are many little hillocks, mounds and dunes around here, some revealing traces of stonework and it has long been assumed to be the site of a pre-reformation Kirk. The name itself can be translated from Norse as meaning a holy or sacred site. However there are no significant finds or written sources that support this idea and it's perfectly possible that the sacred place referred to was a pre-Christian (pagan) site, of which the name alone has survived into the Christian era (verdict – unlikely).

The HOLM OF AIKERNESS is a skerry (virtually three skerries at high tide) which lies just off Westray's north east coast (opposite the airfield) and is almost joined to its larger neighbour at low tide. It's said that a chapel (complete  with chancel and nave and still partially standing in the 17th century) stood in the middle of this barren rock and marked the grave site of seven sisters who were all in monastic orders. The only residents these days are some (seaweed eating) Holmie sheep and the low stone walls that can be seen provide some very basic storm shelter for them, rather than representing chapel remains. Likewise, the stone built shed is a contemporary store.

If anything was here it must have been an incredibly windswept site to choose, even given that the bay may well have been more sheltered then. High seas can swamp the whole skerry and it's not unknown even for the hardy and sure-footed sheep to be swept away during a storm. If a chapel did exist it's likely that the current sheep shelter has been built over it (possibly using some of the stone) as there's really nowhere else a building of that size could go (verdict – likely).

The farm of **NOUP** is the last (inhabited) house before Noup Head and nestles in a steep valley at the head of a small north-facing bay. It's another of these places where a chapel of some description is reported to have been sited but one that at best has several question marks hanging over it. Although there are archaeological remains here suggesting settlement over quite a period of time, nothing has (of yet) been found that supports the story of a chapel. There is no evidence either to suggest that the area was ever particularly populous and whilst that alone doesn't rule out the presence of a medieval chapel, it certainly raises doubts (verdict – unlikely).

Heading east from Noup we stop again at **NOLTLAND CASTLE** (see page 34) where another one-time chapel may have existed. The evidence for this is stronger than for some of the other sites in this section as there are various suggestive references, including a mention in the 1500 Rental documents to the Lady Kirk of Noltland. Alongside this was the discovery of building

foundations in the 1920s, around which were uncovered the graves of 75 people. Today there are no obvious traces of either the foundations

or the cemetery but Sarah Jane Gibbon (see bibliography) suggests that the likely site is the prominent rise to the NE of the castle (much of it within the current boundary dyke). If such a Chapel did exist it would most likely have been demolished when the castle was built in the 16th century. If so, there is every likelihood that the stone was reused in the castle's construction (verdict – likely).

Orkney Museums
and Heritage

5,500 YEARS OF HUMAN HISTORY
Our museums and visitor centres interpret this history, from prehistory, through the Picts and Vikings, to the 21st century.

The Orkney Museum, Kirkwall – *a beautiful 16th-century building, containing our main displays, opposite.....*

St Magnus Cathedral – *a stunning building, founded in 1137 and still used today for worship and concerts - a favourite with visitors*

Kirbuster Museum, Birsay – *a central hearth homestead with 16th-century origins, of European importance*

Corrigall Farm Museum, Harray – *a warm welcome, with peat fires and livestock*

Scapa Flow Visitor Centre and Museum, Lyness, Hoy – *tells the importance of Orkney strategically as a base for the British Fleet in both World Wars and since Napoleonic times*

Orkney Wireless Museum, Kirkwall – *more than 600 radio receivers, including a spy radio in a suitcase and hands-on Morse Code machine*

Stromness Museum, Stromness – *Orkney's natural history, explorers and maritime history, and the Hudson's Bay Company*

Fossil and Heritage Centre, Burray – *important display on fossils and Orkney's geology, and simple social history displays*

**We are especially proud of our World Heritage Site –
The Heart of Neolithic Orkney**

**We work closely with Orkney Disability Forum
and pride ourselves on being family friendly**

**We look forward to your visit! For more details, contact us on:
Tel 01856 873535 Fax 871560 email museum@orkney.gov.uk**

Three quarters of a mile or so south of the castle, on the opposite side of the Loch of Burness can be found two fields known variously as CURQUOY, Kirkquoy and even Korkquoy. They lie just north of the farm at Knugdale and stretch from the public road, just south of Breckowall, to the foot of Knucker Hill.

Older records talk of a very large chambered tomb (30 x 15m) in this area which was reportedly destroyed in 1860. Raymond Lamb's excellent survey of 1983 speculates that both the derivation of the place name (Kirkquoy) and the lack of another known chapel in the immediate area suggests that this may well be an ecclesiastical site but there are alternative linguistic explanations (Cuarquoy meaning corn enclosure) and as there is no other evidence at all to support this we'll put it firmly on our speculative shelf (verdict – unlikely).

The house of HELZIE is the tall white building sitting just to the west of Rapness Pier and has been (probably wrongly) suggested as a possible ecclesiastical site. Henry Fraser in The Third Statistical Account writes in 1950 that with the local pronunciation being "helli" (a ruined house called Hellie sits just behind it) it could derive from helgr meaning holy, suggesting that "this would make the site an ecclesiastical foundation". To be fair to Fraser, he then goes on to suggest that alternatives are hella meaning a flat rock or helir meaning a cave and concludes that "in the absence of other evidence of an ecclesiastical settlement at this spot" and being some distance from the nearest cave, hella is the most likely option. Indeed it is virtually certain that the name refers to the flat rocks which are a coastal feature here and doesn't imply any Kirk connection (verdict - highly unlikely).

The farm of CLEAT, at the last bend on the road down to Cleaton House, is a hamlet in itself. Most dominant is the three storey 18th century farmhouse, which was once the primary residence of Westray's Stewart dynasty. A row of cottages (originally for farm workers) forms a little street round the back and there is the assortment of agricultural buildings that you'd expect for a farm of this size and antiquity.

There has long been assumed to be a burial ground and chapel located just a little to the NE of the buildings, where a sizeable mound still marks the site. Various flagstones and traces of walling can still be found in and around the mound. Although there is nothing standing which is obviously from a chapel, it is clear that some building once stood here. Previous excavations have revealed a considerable number of human remains and so it's quite probable that this was indeed the location of a chapel with cemetery (verdict – likely).

Last in this section is the site(s) of KIRBEST and KNOWE OF BURRISTAE, which some reckon are one and the same. Both are sited beyond the end of the B9067 (Westside) road, which itself ends at the junction by Gairy. If you turn right over the small bridge and follow the road through Netherhouse and over the hill you'll end up at Kirbest (effectively a crofting township rather than a single house).

If you head west instead (and over a couple of fields) from Gairy you'll come upon the obvious mound that is the remains of the **BURRISTAE BROCH**. The possible chapel site is between here and the shore, where a low and almost rectangular outline can be seen.

The main reason for suspecting a site in this area lies again in the name (Kirbest probably derives from old Norse meaning Kirk farm). The likeliest site for a chapel appears to be in a field slightly NW of the house called West Kirbest where the ground is very stony (although there are no obvious foundations or building outlines to be seen on the surface). Indeed ploughing here has produced many stones over the years and the tradition that this was the chapel site has been handed down to the present day. The site is below the current road but is right beside the earlier road of which very little trace now remains.

Other sources suggest that the likelier site may be what's now the low and almost rectangular outline of a building just west of the Burristae Broch. It's been speculated that this may be a 12th – 14th century chapel whilst others reckon that it's more plausibly a much older building, probably a dwelling house.

It is quite probable that there would have been a place of worship of some description in this part of the island and there is some anecdotal evidence to support both ideas although the Kirbest site appears to have the stronger claim. Until we know more we can only say that it could be either, it could be both, or it might be none at all. This particular jury leans towards Kirbest, but only just! (verdict – Burristae unlikely, Kirkbest likely).

buyorkney.com

CHURCH OF SCOTLAND – PAPAY PARISH KIRK

Services every Sunday at 2:30pm
You're welcome to join us

eco
congregation

The Kirk is always open

WORSHIPPING, WITNESSING, CARING

Services every Sunday at 11:30am
You're welcome to join us

See local notices
for details of
evening services

The Kirk is always open

Post-Reformation map of Papay

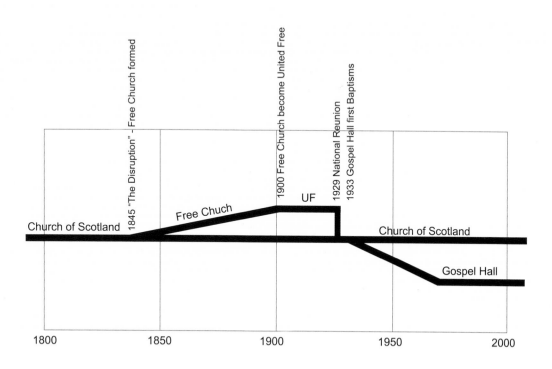

Post-Reformation map of Westray

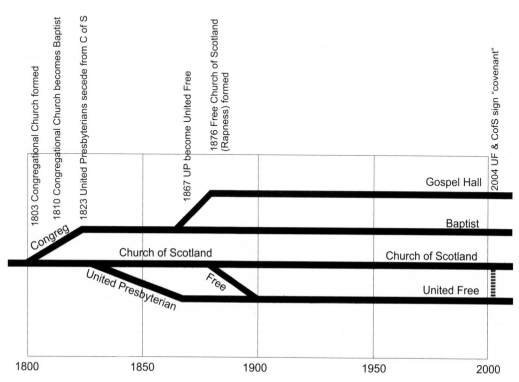

O/S REFERENCES

WESTRAY:

Baptist	HY 435 485
Breckowall	HY 434 482
Brough	HY 448 476
Bu	HY 504 410
Burrian	HY 503 429
Church of Scotland	HY 494 426
Claybraes	HY 443 476
Cleat	HY 464 468
Community Hall & Room	HY 437 484
Cross Kirk	HY 455 431
Curquoy	HY 431 474
East Kirk	HY 456 461
East Chapel	HY 463 458
Havelsey Cottage	HY 437 485
Heatherview	HY 434 482
Helzie	HY 507 405
Holm of Aikerness	HY 469 525
Gospel Hall	HY 437 485
Kalisgarth	HY 438 488
Kirbest	HY 426 437
Knowe of Burristae	HY 430 429
Noltland Castle	HY 429 486
Noltland Chapel	HY 429 487
North Cottohowan	HY 437 438
Noup	HY 412 488
Old Kirkhouse	HY 489 452
Old School, Rapness	HY 499 420
Old School, Skelwick	HY 485 453
Peterkirk	HY 499 400
Rapness Kirks	HY 494 426
Sheepie Kirk	HY 445 468
St. Mary's Kirk	HY 439 488
Trenabie Mill	HY 438 479
UF	HY 445 473
Vestray	HY 446 499
War Memorial	HY 439 489

PAPAY:

Gospel Hall	HY 495 535
Kirk o' Howe	HY 493 531
Papay Community School	HY 494 515
St. Ann's	HY 494 515
St. Boniface	HY 488 526
St. Tredwell	HY 496 508
Via	HY 498 532
War Memorial	HY 489 517

SOURCES AND FURTHER READING.

The following is less of a formal bibliography and more of a reading list for those who are interested in finding out anything further.

Anderson's Guide to Orkney (out of print).

Archaeological Sites and Monuments of Papa Westray and Westray (the) by R G Lamb, RCAHMS, 1983.

Circle of Light : The Catholic Church in Orkney since 1560 by Alison Gray, John Donald, 2000.

Fae Quoy tae Castle by Nancy Scott, Catherine Stevenson and Angie Stout (Eds), Westray Buildings Preservation Trust, 2002.

Heritage of Westray Past, Present and Future (the) by Graeme Wilson and Hazel Moore, Westray Development Trust, 2004.

History of the Orkney Baptist Churches (the) by Henry Harcus, David Hourston,1898.

Kirk in Westray (the) by Elsa Rendall (local publication)

Labour of Love by Iain MacDonald, Westray Parish Kirk, 2002.

Lest We Forget by Elsa Rendall (local publication).

Looking Back by George Drever, 1998, Westray Heritage Trust.

National Gazeteer of Great Britain and Ireland (the), 1868.

Origins and Early Development of the Parochial System in the Orkney Earldom (the) by Sarah Jane Gibbon, unpublished PhD thesis.

Orkney Guide Book (the) by Charles Tait, Charles Tait Photographic, 1991.

Orkney Through the Centuries by D P Thomson, Munro Press, 1956.

Papay by Jocelyn Rendall, Papay Publications, 1992.

Papa Westray Church of Scotland By Jocelyn Rendall & Iain MacDonald, local, 2001.

Papa Westray Farm and House Names by Jim Rendall, (course essay), 1996.

Papay Place Names by John Drever (local – unpublished)

St. Boniface Kirk by Jocelyn Rendall, Papay Publications, 1994.

St. Boniface Church, Orkney (Coastal Erosion and Archaeological Assessment by Christopher Lowe, Sutton, 1998.

The (old) Statistical Account of Scotland Vol XVI (1796)

The New (second) Statistical Account Vol XV (1842)

The Third Statistical Account of Scotland Vol XXA (1950)

Two Millennia of Church and Community in Orkney by Frank D Bardgett, Pentland Press, 2000.

The following web-sites are of direct interest:

GENUKI: www.genuki.org.uk

RCAHMS (The Royal Commission on the Ancient and Historical Monuments of Scotland): www.rcahms.gov.uk

Papar Project: www.rcahms.gov.uk/papar

Orknet: www.orknet.co.uk

INDEX